EMMANUEL JOSEPH

The Carbon Ledger, How Billionaires Are Using Crypto to Build Green Nations

Copyright © 2025 by Emmanuel Joseph

All rights reserved. No part of this publication may be reproduced, stored or transmitted in any form or by any means, electronic, mechanical, photocopying, recording, scanning, or otherwise without written permission from the publisher. It is illegal to copy this book, post it to a website, or distribute it by any other means without permission.

First edition

This book was professionally typeset on Reedsy.
Find out more at reedsy.com

Contents

1	Chapter 1: The New Age of Philanthropy	1
2	Chapter 2: Blockchain for a Greener Planet	3
3	Chapter 3: The Visionaries Behind the Movement	5
4	Chapter 4: Green Crypto Projects Leading the Charge	7
5	Chapter 5: The Economics of Green Cryptocurrencies	9
6	Chapter 6: Regulatory Challenges and Opportunities	11
7	Chapter 7: Tech Giants Joining the Cause	13
8	Chapter 8: Green Finance and Sustainable Investments	15
9	Chapter 9: Case Study - Crypto and Renewable Energy	17
10	Chapter 10: The Role of Decentralized Finance (DeFi)	19
11	Chapter 11: Public Perception and Awareness	21
12	Chapter 12: Overcoming Skepticism and Criticism	23
13	Chapter 13: The Future of Green Crypto	25
14	Chapter 14: Global Collaboration and Partnerships	27
15	Chapter 15: Ethical Considerations and Social Impact	29
16	Chapter 16: Inspiring Stories of Change	31
17	Chapter 17: A Call to Action	33

1

Chapter 1: The New Age of Philanthropy

In the dawn of the 21st century, an unexpected alliance began to form between the world of cryptocurrency and the urgent call for environmental sustainability. Billionaires, traditionally known for their vast wealth and sometimes controversial business practices, started channeling their resources into green initiatives. This chapter explores the roots of this paradigm shift, shedding light on the motivations driving these high-net-worth individuals to invest in green technologies and projects. From Elon Musk's Tesla initiatives to Bill Gates' Breakthrough Energy Ventures, we delve into the groundbreaking efforts to merge innovation with sustainability.

As the effects of climate change became more evident, a sense of urgency permeated the global community. This urgency was not lost on the affluent, who recognized both the ethical responsibility and the financial potential in addressing environmental challenges. For many billionaires, investing in green technologies became more than just a charitable endeavor; it was an opportunity to shape the future and leave a lasting legacy. This chapter examines the personal convictions and strategic foresight that led these individuals to champion the green revolution.

The intersection of wealth and technology has always been a driving force for innovation. In this context, cryptocurrencies emerged as a powerful tool for funding and tracking environmental projects. The decentralized nature of blockchain technology provided a transparent and immutable record, ensuring that funds were used as intended. By leveraging crypto, billionaires could support green initiatives with unprecedented efficiency and accountability. This chapter delves into the technological advancements that facilitated this new age of philanthropy.

Finally, we explore the broader implications of this shift for society. As billionaires harnessed the power of crypto to combat climate change, they also inspired a new generation of entrepreneurs and investors to prioritize sustainability. This chapter highlights the ripple effects of their actions, from influencing policy decisions to fostering a culture of environmental stewardship. The story of how the wealthy elite embraced green crypto initiatives serves as a testament to the transformative power of innovation and the potential for positive change in the world.

2

Chapter 2: Blockchain for a Greener Planet

Blockchain technology, the backbone of cryptocurrencies, offers a transparent and immutable ledger system that has found applications far beyond digital currencies. This chapter examines how blockchain is being leveraged to monitor and verify carbon credits, making the process more transparent and accountable. By utilizing blockchain, companies can ensure that their carbon offset efforts are genuine and traceable, thereby gaining the trust of consumers and investors alike. We delve into real-world examples where blockchain is driving significant environmental change and the potential it holds for the future.

One of the key advantages of blockchain technology is its ability to provide a decentralized and tamper-proof record of transactions. This feature has significant implications for the management of carbon credits, which have traditionally been plagued by issues of fraud and mismanagement. By recording carbon credits on a blockchain, companies can create a transparent and verifiable system that ensures the integrity of their environmental efforts. This chapter explores the technical aspects of blockchain technology and how it is being applied to create more trustworthy and efficient carbon credit systems.

Blockchain's potential to revolutionize carbon management extends beyond mere record-keeping. Smart contracts, a key feature of blockchain technology, enable automated and self-executing agreements that can streamline various aspects of carbon trading and management. For instance, smart contracts can automatically enforce compliance with environmental regulations, reducing the need for manual oversight and intervention. This chapter delves into the innovative applications of smart contracts in the realm of carbon management and the benefits they offer in terms of efficiency and reliability.

The impact of blockchain technology on environmental sustainability is not limited to carbon credits alone. Blockchain's transparency and traceability features can be applied to a wide range of environmental initiatives, from supply chain management to renewable energy projects. By providing a reliable and tamper-proof record of environmental data, blockchain can enhance accountability and promote sustainable practices across various industries. This chapter presents case studies of blockchain-driven environmental initiatives and explores the potential for future applications in creating a greener planet.

3

Chapter 3: The Visionaries Behind the Movement

Behind every significant movement are the visionaries who dare to dream and innovate. This chapter profiles some of the most influential billionaires who are at the forefront of using crypto to build green nations. Figures like Elon Musk, Vitalik Buterin, and Richard Branson are not only investing in sustainable technologies but also advocating for systemic change. We explore their backgrounds, motivations, and the unique approaches they bring to the table. Through their stories, we gain insight into the personal and professional journeys that have shaped their commitment to a greener future.

Elon Musk, a household name synonymous with innovation, has played a pivotal role in merging technology with environmental sustainability. As the CEO of Tesla, Musk has revolutionized the electric vehicle industry, making sustainable transportation a reality for millions. His interest in crypto, particularly Bitcoin, has further amplified his influence in the tech world. Musk's ability to leverage his platforms to promote green initiatives, such as Tesla's investments in renewable energy projects, underscores his visionary approach to creating a sustainable future.

Vitalik Buterin, the co-founder of Ethereum, has also made significant strides in the green crypto movement. Ethereum's blockchain technology has provided a foundation for numerous green projects, including decentralized applications that promote environmental sustainability. Buterin's vision extends beyond mere technological advancements; he actively supports initiatives that leverage blockchain for social good. His commitment to creating a decentralized and inclusive future has inspired many in the crypto community to prioritize environmental and social impact.

Richard Branson, the charismatic entrepreneur behind the Virgin Group, is another key figure in the green crypto movement. Branson's investment in clean energy ventures, such as Virgin Galactic and Virgin Hyperloop, demonstrates his dedication to innovative solutions for a sustainable future. His advocacy for environmental causes, combined with his interest in blockchain technology, has positioned him as a leader in the effort to harness crypto for green initiatives. Branson's ability to blend business acumen with a passion for sustainability sets him apart as a true visionary in the movement.

4

Chapter 4: Green Crypto Projects Leading the Charge

As cryptocurrencies gain mainstream acceptance, several projects have emerged with a focus on environmental sustainability. This chapter highlights some of the most promising green crypto initiatives, such as SolarCoin, a cryptocurrency awarded to solar energy producers, and CarbonCoin, designed to incentivize carbon sequestration efforts. We delve into the mechanics of these projects, how they operate, and their impact on the global push towards renewable energy. By showcasing these pioneering efforts, we illustrate the potential of crypto to drive tangible environmental benefits.

SolarCoin is a prime example of how cryptocurrency can be used to promote renewable energy. By awarding SolarCoins to solar energy producers, this initiative incentivizes the production of clean energy and reduces reliance on fossil fuels. SolarCoin operates on a blockchain platform, ensuring transparency and accountability in the distribution of rewards. This chapter explores the impact of SolarCoin on the renewable energy sector and how it has encouraged the adoption of solar power in various regions.

CarbonCoin takes a different approach by focusing on carbon sequestration efforts. This cryptocurrency is designed to reward activities that remove carbon dioxide from the atmosphere, such as reforestation and soil carbon storage. By creating a financial incentive for carbon sequestration, Carbon-Coin aims to mitigate the effects of climate change and promote sustainable land management practices. This chapter examines the mechanisms behind CarbonCoin and its potential to drive large-scale environmental change.

Other notable green crypto projects include Power Ledger, which uses blockchain technology to enable peer-to-peer energy trading, and the Regen Network, which focuses on regenerative agriculture and ecosystem restoration. These initiatives highlight the diverse applications of cryptocurrency in promoting environmental sustainability. By showcasing these projects, we underscore the potential of green crypto to revolutionize industries and drive positive environmental outcomes.

5

Chapter 5: The Economics of Green Cryptocurrencies

The integration of environmental concerns with cryptocurrency isn't just about philanthropy—it's also about economic viability. In this chapter, we explore the economic implications of green cryptocurrencies and how they can be structured to provide financial returns while promoting sustainability. We examine different models of crypto economics, from proof-of-stake to tokenized carbon credits, and how they can create new financial incentives for green behavior. By understanding these economic underpinnings, we can better appreciate the long-term potential of green cryptocurrencies to reshape industries.

Proof-of-stake (PoS) is a consensus mechanism that aims to reduce the energy consumption associated with traditional proof-of-work (PoW) systems. By requiring validators to hold and stake a certain amount of cryptocurrency, PoS ensures the security and integrity of the blockchain while minimizing its environmental impact. This chapter delves into the mechanics of PoS, its advantages over PoW, and how it can support the growth of green cryptocurrencies. We also explore real-world examples of PoS-based projects and their contributions to sustainability.

Tokenized carbon credits represent another innovative approach to combining cryptocurrency with environmental goals. By tokenizing carbon credits, companies can create digital assets that represent a specific amount of carbon dioxide removed from the atmosphere. These tokens can be traded on blockchain platforms, providing a transparent and efficient market for carbon credits. This chapter examines the benefits of tokenized carbon credits, how they operate, and their potential to drive large-scale carbon sequestration efforts.

The economic viability of green cryptocurrencies extends beyond these two models. We also explore other innovative financial instruments, such as green bonds issued on the blockchain and decentralized finance (DeFi) platforms that focus on sustainability. By highlighting these diverse approaches, we illustrate the potential of green crypto to create new financial incentives for environmentally friendly behavior. This chapter underscores the importance of aligning economic interests with environmental goals to drive meaningful change.

6

Chapter 6: Regulatory Challenges and Opportunities

The rise of green cryptocurrencies has not been without its regulatory hurdles. Governments and regulatory bodies around the world are grappling with how to oversee this emerging sector while fostering innovation. This chapter analyzes the regulatory landscape, highlighting both the challenges and opportunities that come with it. We discuss the role of policymakers in creating a conducive environment for green crypto initiatives and the balance that needs to be struck between regulation and innovation. Through case studies of different jurisdictions, we gain a comprehensive view of the regulatory dynamics at play.

One of the primary regulatory challenges facing green cryptocurrencies is the lack of clear guidelines and standards. As an emerging sector, green crypto operates in a relatively uncharted territory, which can create uncertainty for both investors and developers. This chapter examines the efforts of various regulatory bodies to establish frameworks that support the growth of green crypto while ensuring compliance with existing laws. We also explore the potential risks associated with regulatory gaps and the steps being taken to address them.

While regulatory challenges exist, there are also significant opportunities for innovation and collaboration. This chapter highlights examples of jurisdictions that have adopted progressive regulatory approaches to support green crypto initiatives. By fostering a collaborative environment between regulators, industry stakeholders, and environmental organizations, these jurisdictions have created ecosystems that promote sustainable innovation. We delve into the lessons learned from these successful case studies and the potential for replicating their approaches in other regions.

Regulation is not just about compliance; it's also about creating a level playing field that encourages competition and innovation. This chapter discusses the importance of regulatory frameworks that promote transparency, accountability, and consumer protection. By establishing clear guidelines and standards, regulators can help build trust in green cryptocurrencies and attract more investment into the sector. We explore the role of regulatory sandboxes, public-private partnerships, and international cooperation in shaping the future of green crypto.

7

Chapter 7: Tech Giants Joining the Cause

Beyond individual billionaires, major tech companies have also started to embrace green crypto initiatives. This chapter explores the involvement of tech giants like Google, Microsoft, and IBM in the green crypto space. These companies bring significant resources and expertise to the table, amplifying the impact of green initiatives. We examine their projects, collaborations, and the strategic importance of integrating environmental sustainability into their business models. By understanding the role of these corporate powerhouses, we can see how collective efforts are driving systemic change.

Google has been at the forefront of green technology, investing in renewable energy projects and developing tools to monitor environmental impact. In recent years, the company has also shown interest in blockchain technology and its potential to support sustainability efforts. Google's initiatives, such as Project Sunroof, which uses data to promote solar energy adoption, highlight the company's commitment to a greener future. This chapter delves into Google's green crypto projects and their broader implications for the tech industry.

Microsoft, another tech giant, has made significant strides in integrating environmental sustainability into its business model. The company's commitment to becoming carbon negative by 2030 is a testament to its dedication to combating climate change. Microsoft has also explored the potential of blockchain technology to enhance transparency and accountability in its environmental efforts. This chapter examines Microsoft's green initiatives, including its investments in renewable energy and carbon removal projects, and how blockchain is playing a role in these endeavors.

IBM has a long history of innovation and is no stranger to the green tech space. The company's blockchain platform, IBM Blockchain, has been used to support various environmental initiatives, from supply chain transparency to carbon credit management. IBM's collaborations with environmental organizations and other tech companies demonstrate the power of partnerships in driving systemic change. This chapter explores IBM's green crypto projects and the impact they have had on promoting sustainability within the tech industry.

8

Chapter 8: Green Finance and Sustainable Investments

The financial sector plays a crucial role in the transition to a green economy. This chapter delves into the intersection of green finance and cryptocurrency, exploring how sustainable investments are being made using digital assets. From green bonds issued on the blockchain to investment funds focusing on eco-friendly projects, we look at the innovative financial instruments that are enabling the growth of green industries. By highlighting the role of green finance, we underscore the importance of aligning capital with environmental goals.

Green bonds are a powerful tool for raising capital for environmental projects, and blockchain technology is enhancing their transparency and efficiency. By issuing green bonds on the blockchain, issuers can provide investors with a clear and verifiable record of how funds are being used. This chapter explores the benefits of blockchain-based green bonds, including increased investor confidence and reduced administrative costs. We also examine case studies of successful green bond issuances and their impact on promoting sustainability.

Investment funds focusing on eco-friendly projects are another critical component of green finance. These funds, often referred to as green investment funds or ESG (Environmental, Social, and Governance) funds, allocate capital to projects that promote sustainability and social responsibility. This chapter delves into the role of cryptocurrency in green investment funds, including the use of tokenization to represent ownership in sustainable assets. By highlighting the financial performance and environmental impact of these funds, we illustrate the potential of green finance to drive meaningful change.

Decentralized finance (DeFi) platforms are also playing a role in supporting green initiatives. DeFi platforms enable the creation of decentralized financial products and services, providing a more inclusive and transparent alternative to traditional banking. This chapter explores how DeFi platforms are being used to fund and support eco-friendly projects, from renewable energy installations to sustainable agriculture initiatives. By leveraging the principles of decentralization, DeFi has the potential to create a more inclusive and sustainable financial ecosystem.

9

Chapter 9: Case Study - Crypto and Renewable Energy

Renewable energy is at the heart of the green movement, and cryptocurrency is playing a pivotal role in its expansion. This chapter presents a detailed case study of a crypto-backed renewable energy project. We examine the project's inception, the challenges it faced, and the outcomes achieved. By providing a real-world example, we illustrate the practical applications of crypto in promoting renewable energy and the lessons learned along the way. This case study serves as a blueprint for future projects aiming to harness the power of crypto for environmental good.

The case study focuses on a pioneering project that used blockchain technology to support the development of a solar power plant. The project, initiated by a consortium of tech companies and environmental organizations, aimed to create a transparent and efficient system for funding and managing renewable energy installations. By leveraging blockchain, the project ensured that investments were used as intended and provided stakeholders with a verifiable record of the plant's performance and environmental impact.

One of the key challenges faced by the project was securing sufficient funding to cover the high initial costs of solar power installation. To address this, the consortium issued tokens representing ownership in the solar plant, allowing investors to purchase and trade these tokens on a blockchain platform. This innovative approach provided a new source of capital and attracted a diverse group of investors interested in supporting renewable energy. This chapter explores the mechanics of token issuance, the challenges of regulatory compliance, and the strategies used to attract investment.

The outcomes of the project were impressive, with the solar power plant exceeding its energy production targets and providing a significant reduction in carbon emissions. The transparent and efficient management of the plant, enabled by blockchain technology, inspired confidence among investors and stakeholders. This chapter highlights the key lessons learned from the project, including the importance of collaboration, the potential of blockchain to enhance transparency, and the value of innovative financing mechanisms in promoting renewable energy.

10

Chapter 10: The Role of Decentralized Finance (DeFi)

Decentralized Finance (DeFi) has revolutionized the traditional financial system by providing decentralized alternatives to traditional banking services. This chapter explores how DeFi can contribute to green initiatives by providing funding and financial services to eco-friendly projects. We look at DeFi platforms that are specifically designed to support sustainability and how they can democratize access to green finance. By leveraging the principles of decentralization, DeFi has the potential to create a more inclusive and sustainable financial ecosystem.

DeFi platforms operate on blockchain technology, allowing users to access financial services without the need for intermediaries such as banks. This decentralized approach enables greater transparency, security, and accessibility. For green initiatives, DeFi offers a unique opportunity to raise funds and provide financial services to projects that might otherwise struggle to secure traditional financing. This chapter examines the mechanics of DeFi, including lending, borrowing, and trading, and how these services can be tailored to support sustainability.

One of the key benefits of DeFi for green initiatives is the ability to tokenize assets, making it easier to raise capital and engage a broader base of investors. By tokenizing assets such as renewable energy projects or carbon credits, DeFi platforms can create new markets for sustainable investments. This chapter delves into the process of tokenization, its advantages, and the potential challenges associated with it. We also explore real-world examples of DeFi platforms that have successfully funded green projects through tokenization.

The democratization of finance is another crucial aspect of DeFi's potential to drive environmental change. By removing barriers to entry, DeFi platforms can provide access to financial services for underserved communities and smaller projects. This inclusivity can help ensure that the benefits of green finance are distributed more equitably and that a diverse range of voices is represented in the push for sustainability. This chapter highlights the importance of inclusivity in green finance and the role of DeFi in achieving it.

11

Chapter 11: Public Perception and Awareness

The success of green crypto initiatives depends not only on technology and finance but also on public perception and awareness. This chapter examines the role of education and advocacy in promoting green cryptocurrencies. We discuss the efforts of various organizations, influencers, and media outlets in raising awareness about the environmental benefits of crypto. By understanding the importance of public perception, we can identify strategies to increase adoption and support for green initiatives.

Public perception of cryptocurrencies has been shaped by a mix of enthusiasm, skepticism, and misunderstanding. To foster support for green crypto projects, it is essential to address common misconceptions and highlight the positive environmental impact of these initiatives. This chapter explores the strategies used by advocates to educate the public about green cryptocurrencies, from social media campaigns to educational workshops. We also examine the role of influencers and thought leaders in shaping public opinion and driving awareness.

Organizations dedicated to environmental sustainability have played a significant role in promoting green crypto initiatives. By collaborating with tech companies and crypto projects, these organizations have helped bridge the gap between the environmental and crypto communities. This chapter highlights the efforts of various environmental organizations in raising awareness about the potential of green cryptocurrencies. We also explore the importance of partnerships and collaborations in amplifying the message and reaching a broader audience.

Media coverage is another critical factor in shaping public perception of green cryptocurrencies. Positive media coverage can help build credibility and trust, while negative coverage can hinder adoption and support. This chapter examines the role of media in promoting green crypto initiatives, including the challenges of combating misinformation and the importance of accurate reporting. By understanding the dynamics of media coverage, we can develop strategies to effectively communicate the benefits of green cryptocurrencies.

12

Chapter 12: Overcoming Skepticism and Criticism

Despite the potential benefits, green cryptocurrencies face skepticism and criticism from various quarters. This chapter addresses the common concerns and misconceptions surrounding green crypto, such as energy consumption and environmental impact. We provide a balanced view, presenting both the criticisms and the counterarguments that highlight the positive contributions of green crypto. By engaging in constructive dialogue, we can better understand the complexities of the issue and work towards more sustainable solutions.

One of the primary criticisms of cryptocurrencies is their energy consumption, particularly in the case of proof-of-work (PoW) systems like Bitcoin. Critics argue that the energy-intensive nature of mining operations undermines the environmental benefits of green crypto initiatives. This chapter examines the validity of these concerns and explores the steps being taken to address them. We discuss the shift towards more energy-efficient consensus mechanisms, such as proof-of-stake (PoS), and the potential for renewable energy-powered mining operations.

Another common criticism is the perceived lack of regulation and oversight in the crypto space, which can lead to concerns about fraud and mismanagement. This chapter explores the regulatory challenges facing green cryptocurrencies and the efforts to establish transparent and accountable systems. We discuss the importance of robust regulatory frameworks in building trust and credibility and the role of policymakers in supporting the growth of green crypto initiatives.

The environmental impact of blockchain technology extends beyond energy consumption, encompassing factors such as e-waste and resource extraction. Critics argue that the production and disposal of hardware used in mining operations contribute to environmental degradation. This chapter addresses these concerns and highlights the efforts to develop more sustainable hardware and recycling practices. By presenting a balanced view, we aim to foster constructive dialogue and identify potential solutions to the environmental challenges associated with cryptocurrencies.

13

Chapter 13: The Future of Green Crypto

As we look to the future, the potential of green cryptocurrencies to drive environmental change is immense. This chapter explores the emerging trends and innovations that are shaping the future of green crypto. From advancements in blockchain technology to new regulatory frameworks, we examine the factors that will influence the trajectory of green cryptocurrencies. By anticipating future developments, we can better prepare for the opportunities and challenges that lie ahead.

Advancements in blockchain technology, such as the development of more energy-efficient consensus mechanisms and scalable solutions, will play a crucial role in the future of green crypto. This chapter examines the latest technological innovations and their potential to enhance the environmental sustainability of cryptocurrencies. We also explore the role of research and development in driving these advancements and the importance of continued investment in green tech.

New regulatory frameworks will also shape the future of green cryptocurrencies. As governments and regulatory bodies gain a better understanding of the crypto space, we can expect more comprehensive and supportive policies to emerge. This chapter discusses the potential regulatory developments and their implications for green crypto initiatives. We also highlight the importance of proactive engagement with policymakers and the need for industry collaboration to advocate for favorable regulatory environments.

The future of green crypto will be influenced by the broader trends in environmental sustainability and social impact. As awareness of climate change and the need for sustainable practices grows, we can expect increased interest and investment in green crypto projects. This chapter explores the potential for green cryptocurrencies to become a mainstream component of the global push towards sustainability. By aligning with broader environmental and social goals, green crypto can drive meaningful change and create a more sustainable future.

14

Chapter 14: Global Collaboration and Partnerships

The fight against climate change is a global endeavor, and green crypto initiatives are no exception. This chapter highlights the importance of international collaboration and partnerships in advancing green crypto projects. We look at examples of cross-border initiatives and the role of international organizations in facilitating cooperation. By fostering a spirit of collaboration, we can amplify the impact of green crypto on a global scale.

International organizations such as the United Nations and the World Economic Forum have recognized the potential of green cryptocurrencies to drive sustainable development. By partnering with tech companies, governments, and non-profits, these organizations can create a coordinated approach to environmental challenges. This chapter explores the role of international organizations in promoting green crypto initiatives and the benefits of a collaborative approach. We examine case studies of successful cross-border projects and the lessons learned from these efforts.

Cross-border initiatives often face unique challenges, such as regulatory differences, cultural barriers, and logistical complexities. However, the potential benefits of international collaboration can far outweigh these challenges. This chapter delves into the strategies used to overcome these obstacles and the importance of building trust and cooperation among diverse stakeholders. By highlighting the successes and challenges of cross-border projects, we provide insights into the best practices for fostering global collaboration.

Partnerships between the public and private sectors are also crucial for the success of green crypto initiatives. Governments can provide the regulatory support and funding needed to scale up projects, while private companies bring innovation and expertise to the table. This chapter explores the role of public-private partnerships in advancing green crypto initiatives and the potential for collaboration to drive systemic change. By showcasing examples of successful partnerships, we illustrate the power of collective action in addressing environmental challenges.

15

Chapter 15: Ethical Considerations and Social Impact

The ethical implications of using cryptocurrency for environmental purposes cannot be overlooked. This chapter delves into the ethical considerations and social impact of green crypto initiatives. We discuss the importance of ensuring that these projects are inclusive, equitable, and socially responsible. By addressing ethical concerns, we can build a more just and sustainable future for all.

One of the key ethical considerations is the potential for green crypto initiatives to exacerbate existing inequalities. For example, the energy consumption associated with cryptocurrency mining can disproportionately impact vulnerable communities and contribute to environmental degradation. This chapter examines the steps being taken to mitigate these risks, such as the use of renewable energy for mining operations and the development of more energy-efficient technologies. By addressing these ethical concerns, we can ensure that green crypto projects contribute to a more equitable and sustainable future.

Another important ethical consideration is the need for transparency and accountability in green crypto initiatives. To build trust and credibility, it is essential to provide clear and verifiable information about the environmental impact of these projects. This chapter explores the role of blockchain technology in enhancing transparency and accountability, as well as the importance of third-party verification and reporting. By promoting transparency, we can ensure that green crypto initiatives are held to the highest ethical standards.

The social impact of green crypto initiatives extends beyond environmental sustainability to include issues such as social justice, community empowerment, and economic development. This chapter highlights the potential for green crypto projects to create positive social change, from providing financial services to underserved communities to supporting local economies through renewable energy projects. By aligning environmental and social goals, we can create a more holistic approach to sustainability that benefits all members of society.

16

Chapter 16: Inspiring Stories of Change

Throughout the journey of green cryptocurrencies, there are numerous inspiring stories of individuals and communities making a difference. This chapter showcases some of these stories, highlighting the transformative impact of green crypto on people's lives. From small-scale farmers using blockchain to track sustainable practices to entrepreneurs launching innovative eco-friendly startups, we celebrate the positive change brought about by green crypto.

One inspiring story is that of a group of small-scale farmers in Kenya who have embraced blockchain technology to improve their agricultural practices. By using a blockchain platform to track and verify sustainable farming methods, these farmers have been able to access new markets and receive higher prices for their produce. This chapter explores how the adoption of blockchain has empowered these farmers, improved their livelihoods, and promoted sustainable agriculture in the region.

Another inspiring example is an entrepreneur in India who launched a green startup focused on recycling electronic waste. By using blockchain to ensure transparency in the recycling process, the startup has been able to gain the trust of consumers and investors. This chapter delves into the challenges and successes of the startup, highlighting the innovative use of blockchain to promote environmental sustainability and social impact. The story serves as a testament to the power of green crypto to drive positive change at the grassroots level.

We also highlight the story of a community in Brazil that has leveraged green cryptocurrency to fund renewable energy projects. By creating a local cryptocurrency backed by renewable energy credits, the community has been able to attract investment and support the development of solar power installations. This chapter examines the impact of this innovative approach on the community's energy independence, economic development, and environmental sustainability. The story illustrates the potential of green crypto to empower communities and create lasting change.

17

Chapter 17: A Call to Action

In the final chapter, we reflect on the insights gained throughout the book and issue a call to action. We emphasize the importance of collective effort and individual responsibility in building a sustainable future. By harnessing the power of green cryptocurrencies, we can drive meaningful environmental change and create a better world for future generations. The journey towards green nations is a long and challenging one, but with determination and innovation, we can achieve it together.

The transition to a green economy requires the active participation of all stakeholders, from governments and corporations to individuals and communities. This chapter underscores the importance of collaboration and partnership in driving environmental sustainability. We call on policymakers to create supportive regulatory frameworks, businesses to prioritize sustainable practices, and individuals to adopt eco-friendly behaviors. By working together, we can create a more sustainable and equitable future for all.

Green cryptocurrencies have the potential to play a pivotal role in this transition, but their success depends on continued innovation, investment, and advocacy. This chapter highlights the need for ongoing research and development to improve the environmental performance of blockchain technology and create new solutions for sustainability. We also emphasize the importance of raising awareness and building public support for green crypto initiatives. By fostering a culture of sustainability, we can ensure that green cryptocurrencies become a mainstream component of the global effort to combat climate change.

The journey towards green nations is not without its challenges, but the potential rewards are immense. By harnessing the power of green cryptocurrencies, we can drive systemic change, promote environmental justice, and create a better world for future generations. This chapter concludes with a call to action, urging readers to join the movement and contribute to the creation of green nations. Together, we can turn the vision of a sustainable future into reality.

In "**The Carbon Ledger: How Billionaires Are Using Crypto to Build Green Nations**," explore the groundbreaking convergence of cryptocurrency and environmentalism. This illuminating book reveals how some of the world's wealthiest individuals are leveraging the power of blockchain technology to drive sustainability and create a greener future. From Elon Musk's ambitious ventures to Bill Gates' investment in clean energy, discover the visionary efforts that are reshaping our planet.

Dive into the intricacies of blockchain and its applications in carbon credit management, renewable energy projects, and decentralized finance. Learn about innovative green crypto projects like SolarCoin and CarbonCoin, and understand the economic, regulatory, and technological challenges and opportunities they face. Through in-depth profiles of leading tech giants and billionaire visionaries, uncover the motivations and strategies behind their commitment to environmental stewardship.

"The Carbon Ledger" not only highlights the transformative impact of green cryptocurrencies but also addresses the skepticism and criticism surrounding them. With real-world case studies and inspiring stories of change, this book offers a comprehensive and balanced view of the potential of green crypto to drive meaningful environmental progress.

www.ingramcontent.com/pod-product-compliance
Lightning Source LLC
LaVergne TN
LVHW020458080526
838202LV00057B/6027